# When ELEPHANTS Listen with THEIR FEET

Discover Extraordinary Animal Senses

Emmanuelle Grundmann • Clémence Dupont
Translated by Erin Woods

For most humans, sight is the first sense we use when we get up in the morning. Our eyes show us a world of shapes and colors. But not all animals see the way we do. Some only detect silhouettes; others live in a world of black and white; and a few live in darkness so deep they don't need sight at all.

## SPECIALIZED EYES

Spiders don't take any half-measures. Plenty of species have eight eyes, one for each of their eight legs. Among **jumping spiders**, the two central eyes see in color, including ultraviolet color (see "Light!" below). The lateral eyes (the ones on the sides) are less sensitive to color but have a wide field of vision that lets them spot the movements of predators far to either side.

## A vertebrate eye: the light decoder

The eye is an incredible machine capable of capturing photons, which are the tiny elementary particles of light. The eye allows photons to enter through the pupil, transmits their message to the retina, then sends the result to the brain using an express highway called the optic nerve. As a result, the image of what the eye sees is formed in the mind.

retina

pupil

optic nerve

## LIGHT!

The light you see comes from the sun. It travels 186,000 miles per second (300,000 kilometers), which is the fastest speed possible. This light, which appears white to us, is actually composed of all the colors of the rainbow, from red to violet. In fact, humans only see the part of it we call "visible light." The sun sends other rays to us that our eye doesn't capture, like ultraviolet rays. These are the famous "UV rays" that cause sunburns.

## THE THIRD EYE

The tuatara, an unusual little reptile found only in New Zealand, has been around since the time of the dinosaurs! When they first hatch, baby tuatara have a third eye on the tops of their heads. By the time the babies reach six months, the eye is covered in scales and can no longer be seen. Nobody knows exactly what its purpose is.

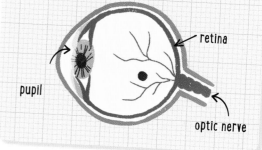

## WHO NEEDS TO SEE?

Zigzagging under the sand of the Southern African desert, the **golden mole** knows only darkness. Eyes? it doesn't have any. They were not useful to the mole's ancestors in this dark underground place, so evolution did away with them. The golden mole "sees" with its ears, detecting the smallest vibration in the sand dunes.

## THE HIDDEN COLORS OF FLOWERS

Sunflower petals look plain yellow to us. But to **bees**, these and other flowers are covered in ultraviolet patterns that are invisible to human eyes. The patterns act as landing strips, guiding bees straight to the sweet source of nectar.

## RECORD

With a diameter of 11.8 inches (30 centimeters), about the size of a human head, the eye of the colossal squid is the biggest in the animal world. These sea creatures have ten pairs of tentacles and can grow to be 17.7 feet long (5.4 meters). They use their giant eyes to spot deep-sea fish and avoid sperm whales, their predators.

## TURN, TURN ABOUT

Our eyes have synchronized movements. That is, they both look in the same direction at the same time. Chameleons, on the other hand, have independently moving eyes that can watch what's going on above and below them at the same time. This is very useful for a slow-moving creature that has to keep a constant lookout for danger.

## THE FLY'S EYES

**Insects** and **crustaceans** have surprising eyes. They are made up of many facets, called ommatidia, that look like miniature camera lenses. Each "lens" captures light and transforms it into a message for the brain. The individual messages are then translated and assembled into a whole image. The more facets the eye contains, the more precise the final image. No wonder it's so hard to catch a **fly**!

## A SEE-THROUGH HEAD!

The barreleye is a strange fish that lives in the night-dark depths of the ocean. It has two huge eyes inside a transparent head dome, which is filled with a gel that protects the eyes against the pressure of the deep ocean. The barreleye can look forward, but its eyes also turn upward to watch for the faint shapes of prey passing between it and the distant surface.

## THE LANGUAGE OF LIGHT

On a warm summer night, two **fireflies** want to meet. To send a message, they create a light at the tips of their abdomens and flash a particular pattern. Among certain species, the female has no wings and looks more like a larva than an adult beetle. Males and females both glow, but beware of imposters: females from the genus *Photuris* are known to imitate the patterns of their neighbors in order to attract and devour them.

## Seeing in the Dark

In the darkness, two eyes are glowing. It's a fox... the backs of his eyes are covered with a particular membrane, the tapetum lucidum. Like a mirror, this membrane captures the tiniest ray of light and bounces it to the retina. This allows the fox to find his way perfectly well on nights when humans can't see anything. This trait is shared by cats, badgers, and the tiny primates in the tarsier family.

ALL EARS

Hearing is essential to the lives of many animals. It allows them to communicate with their neighbors, to find their meals, and to escape from danger. Most animals have a sense of hearing, but they don't all perceive every kind of sound. And not all animals hear with ears as humans do.

## LONG-DISTANCE GOSSIPS

In addition to their famous trumpeting, elephants communicate through strange gurgling sounds. These are infrasound, too low for humans to hear, but they can travel for miles. Elephants walk long distances but keep close family ties, so this long-distance communication allows them to keep in touch with sisters, aunts, and parents.

## What is sound?

When you strike a drum, the drum's skin ripples and a sound emerges. You have created a vibration that will travel through the air all the way to your audience's ears. The faster the vibration is, the higher the sound. We call this the sound's frequency, which is measured in units called hertz. When the sound has fewer than 20,000 vibrations per second (20 hertz), it becomes infrasound. The human ear only hears sounds between 20 and 20,000 hertz. Bats can hear those as high as 80,000 hertz, and elephants can hear sounds as low as 16 hertz.

## WHAT BIG EARS YOU HAVE

"All the better to hear you with," the **fennec** might tell you. Its large ears capture the tiniest sound waves that wander through the Sahara Desert. Hearing is vital for this small fox. Its prey, insects and tiny animals, hide from the desert's burning heat. The fennec finds them by using its sharp hearing to detect even the slightest movements.

## OFFSET EARS

Have you ever amused yourself by covering one ear and then trying to pinpoint the source of a sound? It's not easy. That's because the very brief delay between the arrival of a sound in your right and left ears is what lets your brain identify the direction from which it came. Some kinds of **owl** have perfected this technique; their right ear is slightly larger and higher than the other. In addition, the feathers on these owls' heads create a kind of parabolic antenna that catches sound and funnels it in to the ears.

## AN ANTENNA FOR LISTENING

**Mosquitoes** don't have ears. They use antennae instead. The males' antennae are covered with many fine hairs that are especially sensitive to one particular vibration: they can identify sounds at 380 hertz, which is the frequency emitted by female mosquitoes in flight.
A chance to find love on a summer night…

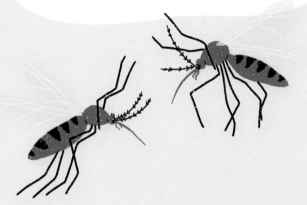

## CROAK, CROAK

The little round disc behind a **frog**'s eye is its eardrum. It's a membrane that captures sound vibrations and transmits them to an inner ear. Each species of frog has a different size and shape of eardrum that is sensitive to a different sound frequency (see the inset on page 7). A clever way to avoid eavesdropping on the neighbors! And in order to make themselves heard, some frogs have an incredible sound box: a vocal sac that they fill with air in order to amplify their voices. Clever!

The blue whale wins the prize for the loudest species on the planet. The sounds it makes can reach 188 decibels, which is louder than the sound of a rocket taking off. If a whale sings near the Canary Islands off the north-western coast of Africa, it can be heard off the eastern coast of North America.

## ECHOLOCATION

In the dark of night or in the depths of the ocean, it can be hard to find your way without bumping into things. Animals like **bats**, dolphins, and even some birds use sonar, which is a powerful and sophisticated tool for navigating. They make a sound and then listen for its echo. Based on the intensity of the echo and the length of time it takes to return, the animal can "see" the obstacles around it. The icing on the cake is that this sonar helps them find prey too, including tiny flying insects.

## TOOT! TOOT!

The **Atlantic herring** is a strange fish. It passes gas to communicate with its neighbors. Small air bubbles are emitted from its anus, making high-pitched bursts of noise in the ocean. It seems that these sounds help shoals of herring stay grouped together during the night when they cannot see each other.

## ULTRASONIC FROG

Originally from China, **odorous frogs** live on noisy stream banks. In order to be heard by their neighbors, the frogs can make and hear ultrasounds (sounds that are too high to be heard by human ears). As far as we know, they are the only amphibians with this ability.

ON
THE NOSE

Humans don't detect a wide range of smells with our 5 million odor-detecting cells. But to dogs, which have about 230 million, the world is bursting with scent! Smells travel long distances through air and water, allowing animals to send messages to mark their territories, find partners, or locate their next meal.

## WILD HUNTERS

**African wild dogs** live on the savannas of Zimbabwe in Africa. These spotted canines are expert at hunting in groups. At dawn or dusk, a small team will go out seeking an antelope. They don't need to see the antelope, and they don't need to worry about staying hidden while they find it; they can pinpoint their prey by smell from up to 1.2 miles (2 kilometers) away. African wild dogs can also chase down their prey for several miles at a speed of about 50 miles (80 kilometers) per hour.

## SMELL TO THE MAX

In proportion to its body, a **bear**'s brain is three times smaller than a human's. However, the part of its brain dedicated to smell is five times more significant than ours. In an all-white environment like the Arctic, it can be hard to find prey using eyesight. But a polar bear can smell a seal more than 19 miles (30 kilometers) away, even if it's under a meter of ice.

### Overlapping Senses

Have you ever noticed that you can't taste things as well when you have a cold? As humans we usually consider scent and taste to be separate, but they are closely linked for us and for many other animals. And while mammals only smell with their noses, insects use their antennae and snakes use their tongues.

11

## AN ALL-PURPOSE TRUNK

**Elephants'** trunks developed when their noses lengthened and merged with their upper lips. Today a trunk can weight more than 220 pounds (100 kilograms). It contains more than 100,000 muscles but no bones, and is extremely flexible and precise. It's a multi-purpose tool with which the elephant can smell odors, pluck a single piece of grass from the savanna, spray itself with water to cool down, or scratch its back with a branch. It can even make music with its trunk or use it as a snorkel to breathe while under water. Imagine if you could do all those things with your nose...

## PERFUME DEER

Scent glands are small pouches inside some animals' bodies where they produce smelly chemicals. The **musk deer**'s scent gland is in its abdomen. A male adult produces about an ounce (30 grams) during the mating season and smears it onto trees to signal his presence to females. Unfortunately, this "musk" is highly sought-after by perfume makers, and the little deer is now on the brink of extinction.

## A BATTLE OF STINK

During the mating season, many male animals fight each other to prove their strength to females. **Ring-tailed lemurs** have a different way of competing. They smear their tails with scent from a gland under their forearm, then shake it under their opponent's nose. Usually, one of the males eventually gives up. If not, they may resort to striking each other with their paws and biting.

## HERO RATS

Ziko, like many **Gambian pouched rats**, is a hero. Thanks to his incredible sense of smell, which is 300 times greater than a human's, he can detect mines buried underground. These explosives cause many deaths around the world each year. And while it takes a human a whole day to inspect a patch of ground half the size of a tennis court for mines, Ziko can do it in just thirty minutes!

## PSST! PSST!

Communicating at night is not always simple. To send a love letter, female **little emperor moths** release odors (pheromones). These odors will travel up to 7 miles (11 kilometers) to catch on the antennae of males.

## BLOWING BUBBLES

The **water shrew** can't see any farther than the tip of its own nose. But who needs to see when you have such a good sense of smell? These shrews can even smell underwater! They blow bubbles from their noses, letting them capture scents from the surrounding water. Then they breathe the bubbles back in and decode the scent messages they now contain.

## THE SCENT OF WATER

Humans can't use their sense of smell under water. That's not the case for fish. In fact, their sense of smell is particularly strong. A **salmon**, for example, can detect one drop of scent dissolved in a body of water the size of ten Olympic swimming pools. Scent is what allows salmon to find their way back to the river in which they were born, and to which they return to lay their own eggs.

### Earth's Funniest Noses

Whether their purpose is to breathe or to detect smells, mammals have a wide—and sometimes amusing—range of nose shapes.

A platypus has a nose shaped like a duck's bill which it uses to feel its environment.

A proboscis monkey's nose is used to attract a mate.

The saiga antelope's nose is designed to warm up the cold air of its northern desert home.

Bitter, sweet, salty, savory, acidic...all the tastes of nature! Some of them are pleasant, others less so. You use taste to decide if you like eating a new food. Among animals, taste is important for more than just eating. It can also be used to communicate with distant neighbors and even to navigate the world.

## DOUBLE THE TASTE BUDS

**Pigs** and dogs are both contenders for the mammal with the most highly developed sense of taste. Pigs also have the advantage of a very useful tongue with more than 20,000 taste buds—more than twice what we humans have. This sense of taste is vital for pigs, which eat just about everything, because it helps them know if something might be poisonous.

## Geography of a Tongue?

For many years, people believed that certain sections of a human tongue specialized in different tastes; for example, that "sweet" taste buds were all at the tip of the tongue. Today we know that while some areas are more sensitive than others, all tastes can be detected by all parts of the tongue.

## EXTRA-LONG TONGUE

Have you ever tried to touch your tongue to the tip of your nose? It isn't easy. But the **okapi** can do it without effort. It can even lick its own ears. The okapi's tongue is not just long at 12–20 inches (30–50 centimeters); it is also prehensile, meaning that it can pick things up. An okapi can use its tongue to pick stems, leaves, fruits, and mushrooms. Then, when the meal is done, it can lick its whole face clean.

## ANT SPOON

The **tamandua** loves ants and termites. It devours more than 9,000 every day. To unearth the insects that make up most of its diet, the tamandua crisscrosses South America's rain forests, sniffing out ant hills and termite mounds. When it finds one, it uses its powerful clawed paws to make a hole. Then it extends its long tongue up to 16 inches (40 centimeters) into the hole. The tongue is sticky, and once it is covered in insects the tamandua simply has to reel it back in and begin digesting.

## A Built-In Straw

Have you ever watched your cat or dog drink? Their tongue isn't just an excellent taste organ; it's also a useful tool for drinking. As soon as the tongue touches the water, surface tension makes water cling to it. Then the animal draws its tongue back into its mouth, making a tube for the water to flow down—kind of like a straw. Even though dogs and cats use the same technique, dogs make a bigger mess with it. That's because they dip their tongues deep into the water, while cats only touch the surface.

## PUT YOUR TONGUE AWAY

**Woodpeckers** use their extremely long tongues to explore rotting wood, feeling out insect larvae and drawing them back to their mouths. But there's one small problem. Wood peckers spend a lot of time banging their heads against trees, making holes to live in or hunting out their dinners. How to avoid biting their own tongues with their beaks? They do it by storing their rolled-up tongues just below their skulls. Smart!

## RECORD

The tongue of the blue whale—the largest animal that has ever lived—weighs as much as an elephant. That's approximately 3 tons!

## A TINY NECTAR PUMP

The **hummingbird** is a tireless nectar drinker. Flapping its wings at high speeds, it hovers over flowers and plunges its long beak into their centers. The tongue acts as a pump, sucking up nectar until the hummingbird draws it back into its mouth. Every day, hummingbirds swallow up to fourteen times their own body weight in nectar. Imagine if you drank more than 80 gallons (300 liters) of fruit juice! Because it is so tiny and so fast, the hummingbird needs all that nectar to replenish the energy it uses.

## SNACK RADAR

The antennae of **moths** look like tiny feathers. Unlike the straight or club-shaped antennae of butterflies, moth antennae have many branches that help the insects orient themselves at night. The branches are covered in taste receptors, allowing the moth to taste the air and avoid flying into objects—or into the mouth of a hungry predator.

## DRAGON TONGUE

It's the biggest lizard in the world...and one of the most dangerous. **The Komodo dragon** is a hunter. It seeks its prey among the tall grasses of its home islands in Indonesia, then leaps upon them and bites them once. Then it only needs to leave the prey alone and wait, because its saliva contains a venom strong enough to kill even a buffalo or a deer. Once the animal is dead, the Komodo dragon uses its tongue to track the smell of decomposing meat, even if the animal traveled several miles before dying.

## BE AFRAID

The **blue-tongued skink**'s name is well earned. When it feels threatened, the little Australian reptile sticks out its tongue, which isn't just a strange color. It also reflects ultraviolet light (see page 4). When it's flicked quickly, the tongue bounces a flash of blue light at the predator, startling them before they can munch on the skink.

## TASTING THE AIR

Have you ever noticed that **snakes** and lizards spend a lot of time flicking their tongues out and pulling them back in? Their tongues act like a butterfly net, capturing the scent particles that float on the air. Drawn back into the mouth, the tongue brings the smells to an organ called the Jacobson organ, which is right below the nostrils. It decodes the scent particles, allowing the brain to come up with a response, whether it's *Run! There's a predator,* or *Attack! We've found prey.*

## LEGS FOR TASTING

The **crab** has no tongue, but it can still taste. Its legs, pincers, and mouth parts are covered with hairs that capture the smells that drift through water. That's how crabs know when they've got dinner clutched in their pincers. Interestingly, butterflies and flies also taste with their feet. Have you ever watched a fly tapping its feet on a fruit or some animal poop? The fly is using taste to decide if it's standing on its dinner.

SKIN SENSING

Our skin sends non-stop messages to our brain: the softness of a fabric, cold and hot temperatures, a pinch, the pain of an insect bite, or even a gentle kiss. We feel these things through tiny cells under the skin that detect pressure and vibrations. Our hairs help too. But not all parts of the body are as sensitive as others, and every species has a unique sense of touch.

## A FRIENDLY TRUNK

Among humans and chimpanzees, friends shake each other's hands when they meet. **Elephants**, on the other hand, say hello by caressing each other with the tips of their trunks. They also use their sensitive trunks to cuddle their babies when they need comforting.

## SOCIAL CONNECTION AND ECONOMIC EXCHANGE

Among **macaques**, grooming each other is important. For one thing, it feels good. The movement of fingers through fur stimulates the release of happy hormones. It's the perfect way to de-stress, especially after a fight. But there's more to it than that. With macaques, grooming is also a kind of currency. They will trade a massage for a piece of juicy fruit or for a cozy place to sleep at night.

## An Underground Star

Like all moles, the star-nosed mole is nearly blind. But underground, sight isn't as useful as a really good nose...and the star-nosed mole has an extraordinary one. Shaped like a star with many tentacles, the mole's nose is covered in super-sensitive cells. They move constantly, touching everything that gets near the mole. This incredible nose doesn't just allow moles to navigate in pitch darkness. It also helps them to identify their prey in record time: less than 8 milliseconds are needed to find and swallow their dinner.

## ANTENNAE ON THE NOSE

The whiskers of felines are both elegant and useful. They act like antennae, detecting the slightest vibration in the air, and they are extremely sensitive to touch. The **lynx**, along with the leopard, the puma, and even your house cat, uses its whiskers to help get around at night without bumping into anything.

## A GOURAMI HUG

To lay her eggs, the female **gourami** needs to be tickled. But the male won't go ahead and do it without her permission. The female signals him by nibbling at his sides; then he gets into position beneath her and caresses her belly with his fin until the eggs are ready to come out.

## BIRDS DON'T WEAR SOCKS

If you've ever tried to walk barefoot on snow, you probably ran back inside in a hurry to warm up your toes. But **birds** can stand on ice for hours without so much as a shiver. This is because they have no nerve endings in their feet, so they don't feel extreme temperature changes.

## SNUGGLING LIKE A MACAW

**Macaws** are big parrots from the tropical Americas. They spend a lot of time grooming their companions' feathers with their beaks. This practice is important to help the birds maintain the feathers they need to fly, but it also helps strengthen the social bonds between members of a group. As one macaw nudges the feathers of another, that macaw's touch receptors activate and send positive signals to its brain.

## A NOSE AT THE END OF HIS BEAK

The **kiwi** is a strange bird. First of all, it doesn't fly. Second, its nostrils are at the tip of its beak instead of near its base. Then again, this trait is useful for a bird that uses smell and touch to rummage through soil to find worms and insects.

## HAIRY FEET

Although they are often invisible to the naked eye, the bodies of **insects** and many **arthropods** possess tiny hairs. Their feet are covered in them, with each hair connected to a neuron. When the hair moves, a message is sent to the brain and the brain responds with a signal to either run, attack, or woo a mate.

## HOLD THE LINE

Many **fish** swim in shoals to protect themselves from predators. This incredible spectacle of synchronized swimming depends on touch, even if the fish are never in physical contact with each other. Many shoaling fish seem to have a line drawn down the middle of their bodies, and it's not there for show. The line is made of cells that are extremely sensitive to vibrations in the movement of water. As soon as one fish breaks to the right or left, a tiny current forms that is immediately sensed by the cells of the other fish. As a result, the whole shoal can change direction together.

## Take a Beak

Shore birds rely on their sensitive beaks to search the mud for worms, shellfish, and other delicacies. The sense of touch in their beaks is unusual among birds, which usually have their touch receptors in their feathers and skin. Each shore bird's beak is specialized for a certain kind of prey.

The Eurasian oystercatcher specializes in shellfish, which is how it got its name.

The Eurasian curlew searches out worms and molluscs in the shoreline mud.

The avocet skims the surface of the water in search of tiny prey.

The spoonbill uses its large beak to filter prey from the water.

GOOD
VIBRATIONS

When you listen to music, have you ever noticed that you can feel the vibrations of certain low sounds in your body? Do they ever make you shiver? We very rarely use these kinds of low sounds in our communications, but some animals can't manage without them. Whether underground or in the dark of night—anytime it's impossible to see or hear each other— certain animals use vibrations to find their way, to communicate, or to hunt.

## TAP YOUR FEET

An **elephant**'s trumpeting is a familiar sound, but this animal also communicates using low-frequency sounds (see page 7) and foot-stomping. And when a four-ton giant stomps its feet, the whole savannah shakes. These vibrations are mini earthquakes that quickly travel for miles through the ground. Elephants "listen" to these vibrations using sensitive cells in the bases of their feet. A handy way to chat with distant cousins!

## A WHISKER AWAY

Underwater, it's sometimes hard to see past the end of your nose. This doesn't matter to the **manatee**, which gets around with the help of some super-sensitive whiskers. Similarly, on dry land, many other animals use whiskers to find their way at night, including jaguars and many other felines.

## A DRUMMING RAT

Danger is approaching. Quickly, the **kangaroo rat** drums its powerful legs against the ground. The drumming carries to other kangaroo rats in a wide area, warning them to hide. It also signals to hungry snakes that their cover has been blown and they should move on. Rabbits use drumming sounds too, and so do plenty of other rodents that live in underground burrows. This method allows them to communicate with neighbors without leaving the safety of their home.

## TOK TOK. WHO'S THERE?

In the deserts of southern Africa, it can be hard to locate a partner during the mating season. The **tok-tok beetle** has found a solution: it plays a drum solo by striking its abdomen against the ground. As soon as the concert begins, beetles from all around start heading toward the musician.

## WARNING!

The huge mounds built by **termites** are no protection against the claws of an anteater or aardvark, or even against the clever hands of a chimpanzee who is craving a juicy insect snack. As soon as their home is damaged, worker termites strike their heads against the walls in a rhythm of eleven strikes per second. This alarm, once triggered, spreads throughout the whole colony.

## A STICKY TRAP

Ambush hunting takes patience. And it's impossible to get on with your day while you're waiting around for your prey to show up. The **European garden spider**, like many other spiders, has solved this problem by building a trap: a huge silk web. Woven in a strategic spot and nearly invisible, it sticks to any careless critters that stumble into it. The more the insect struggles, the more it gets tangled in the web. The insect's movements also make the web vibrate, alerting the spider that dinner is served.

## SURFING THE SWAMP

Fishing spiders also use vibrations to find their dinner, but they do it in the water. This spider surfs on the surface of swamps and uses its feet to sense the tiniest ripple that might signal the presence of prey.

## SHAKE IT, SNAKE

The name **rattlesnake** refers to an accessory on the tip of this reptile's tail: hollow scales that act like a musical shaker. At each molt, when the snake sheds its old skin, a new row of scales is added to the rattle, making it louder. When they move through the underbrush, the twenty-seven species of rattlesnake —all American and all venomous—make music with their tails to announce their presence.

## A FIDDLE AND A DANCE

The male **fiddler crab** has an inventive way to attract a mate to his seaside burrow. He choreographs a dance, waving his outsized pincer in the air as if to say, "Come visit my ocean-view villa!" Once he catches a female's interest, he backs into his tunnel while giving a drum concert by tapping its walls with his big pincer. The rhythm of the vibrations gives her information about the burrow and about the male's size—the bigger the crab's shell, the closer together the soundwaves.

## RECORD

Who would have thought that a crocodile's muzzle is as sensitive as a human's fingertips? This sensitivity helps crocodiles detect vibrations created by the movements of fish and other prey. They also pick up vibrations emitted by male crocodiles to woo females or to show off to their rivals.

## UNEARTHING THE WORM

Do you know how to summon **earthworms**? Simply by tapping the ground with a stick. This creates vibrations that remind worms of an approaching mole, their greatest predator, so they flee to the surface. Badgers take advantage of this by growling out their own vibrations as they dig with their powerful claws. The worms pop out of the ground and the badger eats them up. In fact, badgers love earthworms so much that they can eat hundreds in one night.

POINTING NORTH

Humans need compasses if they want to navigate using the earth's magnetic field. But some animals can sense the field itself. These globe-trotting creatures don't need a backpack, map, or anything else. Everything they need is in their own head. Just like the needle of a compass, they know exactly where the cardinal points of north, south, east, and west lie. Other species have another superpower: they can sense the electric impulses emitted by their neighbors, and they use them to hunt, to defend themselves, to communicate, and to find their way.

## The Earth's Magnetic Field

The earth is like a huge magnet. In its center, the planet creates a sort of invisible shield that repels harmful rays from the sun. That shield is the magnetic field. It extends thousands of miles into space and determines where the north and south poles are located. The Chinese were the first humans to use the magnetic field by developing compasses. This navigational tool includes a tiny magnetized needle that always points north, attracted to the planet's magnetic field.

## TRIPLE-THREAT MUZZLE

An **echidna**'s muzzle isn't just a mouth and a nose; it's also an electrical signal detector. The long-beaked echidna has 2,000 cells that specialize in this function; the short-beaked echidna, which lives in drier areas, has 400. They both use their detectors to help find termites, mice, and worms to eat.

## MAGNETIC MOUSING

To catch small rodents, **foxes** use a hunting technique called "mousing": they jump high in the air, rounding their back, and land on their prey. Interestingly, foxes always prefer to be facing north-east when they perform this trick—and researchers have shown that foxes that keep to this habit have a much higher chance of success. They think the fox follows the sounds of prey hiding in grass or beneath the snow, then pinpoints exactly how far away they are using their sense of the earth's magnetic field. Sly fox!

## ELECTRO-BILL

The **platypus** is an absurd animal. In fact, for a long time, people thought they were a hoax because even though they are mammals, platypuses lay eggs and have duck-like bills. These bills contain more than 40,000 tiny electroreceptors. Down in the mud of the Australian and Tasmanian rivers where they live, these receptors allow them to sense the electric fields produced by tiny crustaceans, worms, and insect larvae.

# VERSATILE NAVIGATORS

Magnetism isn't just important to migrating birds. It's also used by the largest animals on earth: **whales**. These mammals use several tools to help them navigate: echolocation (see page 9), the positions of the sun and stars, and cells in their heads that are sensitive to the earth's magnetic field. These tools allow whales to travel thousands of miles every year.

# CLIMATE CONTROL

In Australia, **termites** build extraordinary mounds. They are tall, flat and narrow, with their short edges always facing north-south. This isn't an aesthetic choice; it's all about comfort. With the wider edges of the mound facing east where the sun rises and west where it sets, the sun's movement helps to circulate the air inside and keep it to a consistent temperature of 86 degrees Fahrenheit (30 degrees Celsius). This climate-controlled architecture is made possible by these tiny insects' internal compasses.

# BUTTERFLY GPS

The **monarch butterfly** is a traveler. After summering in Canada, it sets out on a trip of more than 3,000 miles. It takes three months to reach the forests of Mexico where it will hibernate and mate. To keep on track, these insects depend on their antennae, which contain tiny magnetic receptors.

# NATURAL COMPASSES

There's more than one way for an animal to read the earth's magnetic field. The internal compasses of bees and trout contain crystals of the mineral magnetite. Like a magnet, it reacts to magnetic variations. **Pigeons** have these crystals in their beaks, but they also have a pigment in their eyes that refines how they detect magnetic north.

# ELECTRIC GENERATOR

The **electric eel** has between 5,000 and 6,000 electroplates (see inset) in its abdomen that can generate a discharge of nearly 600 volts, stunning the eel's prey. The eel can also create weaker electrical currents, about 10 volts, which it uses to navigate.

# MAPPING THE OCEAN

This strange fish, **Peters' elephantnose fish**, creates faint electrical impulses of less than one volt and sends them out through the water. These impulses bounce off objects, warping as they do so. Then they return to the fish's muzzle like a boomerang, and the warped shape of the impulses allows the fish to build a mental map of the area around it. A handy way to navigate, locate food, and even find a mate!

# TORPEDO POWER

The **torpedo** doubles up on its electrical organs: it has one on either side of its head. Take care if you ever encounter this fish, which can discharge between 8 and 200 volts to electrocute its prey or stun a predator.

## Producing Electricity

Humans do create electricity to power our muscles, but we can't sense it. Some animals emit much more powerful electric discharges. They are produced in a specialized organ made up of "electroplates," which are muscle and nerve cells that are modified and chained together to create a kind of giant battery. "Volts" are the units we use to measure electric currents.

# SHARK SENSES

In the vast ocean, the ability to detect electrical signals produced by the muscles of other animals is extremely useful. **Sharks** are particularly good at detecting weak electrical currents, thanks to structures under their skin called "ampullae of Lorenzini."

Superhero
ANIMALS

What powers does your favorite superhero have? Nearly all superpowers were inspired by animals and their incredible skills. Walking on the ceiling, running on water, always landing on their feet, or being nearly immortal... these are just some of the amazing abilities that exist in nature.

# WALKING ON WATER

Need to cross a river to escape a predator? The common basilisk and the **sailfin lizard** simply run across. This incredible ability—one that is not shard by any other vertebrates—has earned them the nickname "Jesus lizards." Here's how it works: The lizard's foot touches the surface of the water. A bubble forms where the water is displaced. The bubble generates enough force to lift the lizard, which bounces forward to take its next step.

# SUCTION-CUP TOES

Have you ever daydreamed about walking on the ceiling? **Geckos** do it easily. The secret to this superpower is in the shape of their feet. Their fingers and toes are enlarged and covered with millions of microscopic hairs. These hairs push into every crack and crevice on even the smoothest surface, allowing the gecko to stick to it like a suction cup. The sticking effect is so strong that smaller geckos can hang by just one finger.

# LANDING ON YOUR FEET

Unlike buttered toast, a falling **cat** always lands right-side up and on its feet. It manages this with cooperation between its sense of sight and its inner ear. Inside the ear, tiny bones help give a sense of balance and tell the cat if it's upside-down. Thanks to its flexible spine, the cat can turn itself over, even in mid-air. Finally, the cat uses its whiskers to measure the distance to the ground, readying itself to bend its legs and absorb the shock of landing. Ten points!

## A MULTI-SENSE MIGRATION

The **bar-headed goose** has an impressive list of exploits: it travels a long distance at heights reaching more than 24,000 feet above sea level when it flies over the Himalayas, a chain of mountains in Asia. Oxygen levels are low at those heights, but the goose isn't bothered. To navigate, it uses the earth's magnetic field, the positions of the stars, and the shape of the landscape. Researchers have also studied whether these geese have a sixth sense that lets them predict earthquakes, but it looks like that's not exactly true. Like some other animals, including elephants and dolphins, they are simply able to sense the faintest tremors that come before a big shake.

## DANCE ALL SUMMER

In the old story, the grasshopper danced and sang all summer while the ant worked. **Bees** dance all summer too, but their fancy footwork isn't just for fun. Each dance communicates an important message: turning in a circle means pollen-rich flowers are near. A figure-eight says the bees will have to fly far—and the dancing bee's position shows them what direction to take. Movements of the bee's abdomen and the speed of its half-turns describe the distance to a meal and its quality.

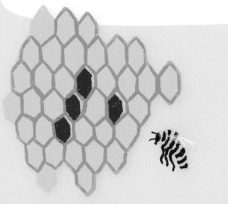

## KEEP LOOKING UP

The **sea star**, like most of us, prefers to be right-side up—even though it doesn't have a head. But far under the ocean, how does it know which way the surface is? The sea star has a specialized organ for that purpose. It contains a cell with a sort of marble loose inside it. As the sea star moves, the marble rolls around and bumps into the cell walls, telling the sea star which way its body is tilted.

## SALAMANDER SURGERY

A **Japanese giant salamander** has lost a toe during a fight with a rival. He doesn't care; he has a super healing power. Certain cells in his body will rapidly seal the wound, then search the memory of the surrounding tissues to find out what they should become. Set program to "foot" mode. It can take a whole year, but the salamander will eventually re-grow his missing piece.

## DISAPPEARING ACT

The **octopus** is a masterful escape artist, able to fit through the tiniest crack. It pulls this off thanks to its flexible, elastic body. It can reshape itself, flatten itself, and flow through a hole less than an inch wide. This is true even of the biggest species, like the giant Pacific octopus, which is more than 14 feet (4 meters) wide. Add to this the octopus' excellent camouflage skills and the cloud of ink it can squirt into the water when it's threatened, and you will understand why so many scientists are fascinated with them.

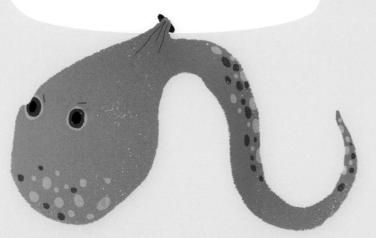

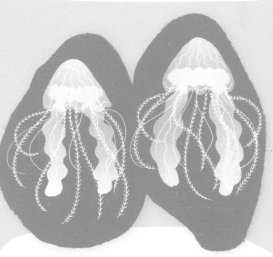

## AGING BACKWARD

*Turritopsis nutricula* is a small animal, just four to five millimeters at most. But this tiny Caribbean **medusa** has achieved something humans only dream of: immortality. Like many other medusas, it begins its life as a polyp (a tiny tube-shaped animal with a crown of tentacles) that spends its time attached to a rock. Polyps enter a stage called "budding" to produce medusas that will give birth to the next generation of the species. But the medusas are also able to change back to their childhood polyp form. This unique ability means this animal can, in theory, be practically immortal.

# INDEX OF ANIMALS

This index lists the animal species mentioned in this book and the pages on which you can find them.

## AMPHIBIANS

### Frogs
There are about 4,800 known species of frogs and toads in the world. But their numbers have been declining alarmingly since the 20th century.
See page 8 and 9

### Japanese Giant Salamander
Japanese giant salamanders are a national treasure of the Japanese archipelago. It has been illegal to hunt them for decades. In fact, it is even illegal to touch them without special authorization. Nevertheless, these amphibians are still threatened by pollution and habitat loss.
See page 33

### Odorous Frogs
There are fifty-seven known species of odorous frogs, all of them in Asia.
See page 9

## ANNELIDS

### Earthworms
There are more than 6,000 known species of earthworm, some of which can reach lengths of up to 3 meters (10 feet). They all eat decomposing plant matter.
See page 25

## ARACHNIDS

### European Garden Spider
There are about 650 species of European garden spiders, all of them weavers of enormous and complex webs.
See page 24

### Fishing Spiders
There are more than 100 species of fishing spiders. They are found in every humid environment in the world, except at the poles.
See page 24

### Jumping Spiders
Jumping spiders form the largest family of spiders, with over 6,080 species. They are distinguished by four pairs of eyes in a particular arrangement.
See page 3

### Spiders
There about 45,700 known species of spiders in the world, every one of them with eight legs.
See pages 3 and 24

## CNIDARIANS

### Medusa
Medusa have been around for more than 600 million years and have divided into more than a thousand species. They live in every kind of marine habitat.
See page 33

## CRUSTACEANS

### Crabs
Like all crustaceans, crabs have ten legs and four antennae. We have cataloged more than 6,800 species, of which 850 live in fresh water or on land. The rest live in the ocean.
See page 17

### Fiddler Crabs
There are about 100 known species of fiddler crabs living near tropical mangrove forests.
See page 25

## ECHINODERMS

### Sea Stars
There are about 1,500 known species of sea star. They live throughout the oceans from the poles to the tropics.
See page 32

## INSECTS

### Bees
Like all insects, bees have three pairs of matching legs. There are more than 20,000 known species living everywhere that flowers bloom.
See pages 4, 22, and 28

### Fireflies
There are about 2,000 known species of firefly. They are one of four families of bioluminescent beetles found on every continent; in all, about 12,000 species of beetles make their own light.
See page 5

### Flies
Flies belong to a family of more than 4,000 species and to the order Diptera, which includes more than a million species characterized by their single set of wings. In a fly's short life (about thirty days for the house fly), it can lay up to 500 eggs.
See page 21

### Little Emperor Moth
This moth has a larger cousin, the giant emperor moth.
See page 13

### Monarch Butterfly
This large migrating butterfly saw its population decline so much it was declared endangered in Canada.
See page 28

## Mosquitoes

Mosquitoes belong to the same order as flies, Diptera. There are more than 3,500 mosquito species around the world.
See page 16

## Moths

There are thousands of moth species, most of them active at night, but the artificial lights of our cities change their behaviors and their populations are declining.
See page 20

## Termites

There are more than 3,000 known species of termite, most of which live in the subtropics.
See pages 24 and 28

## Tok-Tok Beetles

There are over 400,000 species of beetle, including the tok-tok beetles that live in the desert of Namibia.
See page 24

# MARINE MAMMALS

## Manatees

There are two manatee species, both belonging to the seal family. One lives in the Southern Ocean and the other the Pacific Ocean off the coast of North America.
See page 23

## Blue Whale

The blue whale is the largest animal alive today. It is in danger of extinction because of past hunting that reduced their population dramatically.
See pages 9 and 16

## Whales

The fifteen species of baleen whale belong to the order Cetacea. Many are in danger of disappearing.
See page 28

# LAND MAMMALS

## African Wild Dog

The African wild dog belongs to the family of canidae, just like wolves and dogs. It's a species in danger of disappearing: at the beginning of the 20th century, there were nearly 500,000 individuals, and now there are fewer than 3,000.
See page 11

## Bats

There are more than 1,200 known species of these flying, nocturnal mammals in the world.
See pages 7 and 9

## Domestic Cat

The domestic cat belongs to the family of small felines (felinae) including pumas, lynx, and ocelots. Your pet cat is a descendent of wildcats.
See pages 16, 19, and 31

## Echidnas

The echidna belongs to the monotreme group of animals (like the platypus) and lives in Australia and New Guinea. There are only four living species of echidna, and they are in critically endangered.
See page 27

## Elephants

There are three species of elephants, two in Africa and one in Asia. Their populations fell from several million in the 1970s to a few hundred thousand today. It's estimated that the species living in the forests of Africa will have disappeared by 2025.
See pages 7, 12, 16, 19, and 23

## Felines

There are about forty-one species of felines in existence today, of which fifteen are in danger of disappearing. We distinguish the small felines, or felinae (domestic cat, lynx etc.), from the large ones, or pantherinae (panther, lion etc.).
See page 19

## Fennec

The fennec is the smallest member of the canidae family, which includes wolves, dogs, and foxes. It lives only in the deserts of northern Africa.
See page 7

## Fox

There are twenty-four known species of fox adapted to a variety of habitats (forest, plain, mountain). Some, like the corsac fox and the Bengal fox, are in danger of extinction.
See pages 5 and 27

## Gambian Pouched Rat

This large rodent lives in the savannas and forests south of the Sahara.
See page 12

## Grant's Golden Mole

This African mole is found only in the Namib and Kalahari Deserts.
See page 4

## Kangaroo Rat

In the kangaroo rat's genus *Dipodomys*, there are twenty species all living in desert habitats.
See page 23

## Lynx

There are four species of this feline: two in central Europe and central Asia, and two in North America. Long hunted for their fur, lynx are protected today.
See page 19

## Macaque
This primate lives in Asia from Japan to India, and in northern Africa. There are twenty-three known species.
See page 19

## Musk Deer
The seven species of this deer, which are found in Siberia, the Himalayas, and Tibet, are in danger of extinction.
See page 15

## Okapi
This ruminant mammal belongs to the same family as giraffes and lives only in a small area of tropical forest in the Democratic Republic of the Congo, in Africa. It has been on the list of endangered species for several years.
See page 15

## Pigs
The domestic pig is a subspecies of boar. Humans domesticated them about 10,000 years ago.
See page 13

## Proboscis Monkey
This monkey is found only on the island of Borneo. Threatened by habitat loss, there are only about 5,000 proboscis monkeys left today.
See page 12

## Platypus
Like the echidna, this mammal lays eggs and belongs to the group monotreme. It lives in Tasmania and Australia, where it is a protected species.
See pages 13 and 27

## Polar Bear
The largest bear in the world lives only at the North Pole and in the Arctic Ocean. Its survival depends on the stability of the arctic ice floes.
See page 11

## Ring-Tailed Lemur
The ring-tailed lemur is not a monkey, but a primate belonging to the family lemuridae. They are found only on the island of Madagascar.
See page 12

## Saiga Antelope
Today, this species of antelope is found only on the steppes and in the deserts of central Asia, where it is also in danger of disappearing.
See page 13

## Star-Nosed Mole
The mole family includes forty-two species spread across Asia, North America, and most of all Europe. They like humid and marshy soils.
See page 19

## Tamanduas
These cousins of the anteater include two species which live in the trees of Mexico, the Amazon rainforest, and other parts of South America.
See page 15

## Water Shrews
These excellent swimmers have spread across all of Europe and Asia.
See page 13

## MOLLUSKS

## Colossal Squid
The heaviest of all molluscs, the colossal squid is even more imposing than the giant squid. It lives in the depths of the Southern Ocean.
See page 4

## Octopuses
The octopus is a mollusc that first appeared 540 million years ago. It has eight arms covered in suckers and it is known for being particularly intelligent.
See page 33

## BIRDS

## Bar-Headed Goose
This wild migratory goose flies over the Himalayan Mountains each year, meeting up in huge colonies in Mongolia and in China.
See page 32

## Eurasian Curlew
Along with its seven close cousins, the Eurasian curlew belongs to the scolopacidae family of shorebirds, most of which are migratory.
See page 21

## Eurasian Oystercatcher
There are twelve species of oystercatchers, but some are endangered.
See page 21

## Hummingbirds
Hummingbirds range in size from 6 inches (15 centimeters) to just 2 inches (5 centimeters) for the bee hummingbird, the smallest bird in the world. There are approximately 340 species of hummingbird, all found in the Americas. Their habitats range from forests to mountains.
See page 16

## Kiwi
This bird lives in New Zealand where it is threatened mainly by predators like dogs,

cats, and rats that were introduced by colonists in the nineteenth century.
See page 20

## Owls
Owls are nocturnal birds of prey. There are more than 200 species of owls living from the Arctic to the tropics.
See page 8

## Pigeons
Pigeons and doves make up a family of 343 known species. The pigeon most city-dwellers are familiar with is called the rock dove.
See page 28

## Shore Birds
There are four species of shore bird living in coastal areas of Europe, Africa, Australia, and America.
See page 21

## Spoonbills
Spoonbills are a genus of six species of wading birds, easily recognized by their large, flat beaks.
See page 21

## Woodpeckers
Woodpeckers are a large family of more than 230 species living in wooded zones from temperate regions to the tropics.
See page 16

# FISH

## Atlantic Herring
Atlantic herring live in the cold waters of the Atlantic Ocean and the Arctic Ocean. Their population has been reduced by overfishing.
See page 9

## Barreleye
We have known about barreleyes, also called spook fish, since 1939, but no living specimen was photographed until 2004.
See page 5

## Electric Eel
The only species of its genus, this fish lives in the fresh water of the Amazon.
See page 29

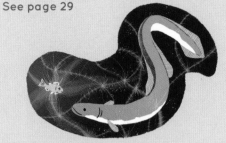

## Gourami
There are 133 known species of this tropical fish, which originate from southeast Asia.
See page 20

## Peters' Elephantnose Fish
The family of this fish, the mormyridae, includes more than 200 species. Each one has the distinction of possessing a brain that is as large as a human's in proportion to their body.
See page 37

## Sharks
In 2014, 529 species of shark had been identified—but most were already endangered due to fishing.
See page 20

## Torpedoes
Also called electric rays, there are about seventy species of this fish living on sandy ocean floors. Some are endangered.
See page 29

## Salmon
There are about ten species of salmon, but studies show that all wild salmon populations are in decline.
See page 13

# REPTILES

## Blue-Tongued Skinks
These lizards live in Australia and Indonesia. They belong to the skink family, which includes more than a million species.
See page 17

## Chameleons
We have cataloged more than 200 species of chameleon. They range from Africa to the Middle-East and in southern Europe.
See page 4

## Crocodiles
There are at least fifteen species of crocodile living in humid tropical regions.
See page 25

## Geckos
Cousins of snakes and lizards, geckos can be found in just about every country and in nearly every climate, except polar regions.
See page 22

## Komodo Dragon
This species of monitor lizard, which lives only on the islands of Indonesia, is endangered due to human activities and the destruction of its habitat.
See page 14

## Rattlesnakes
There are between thirty-two and forty-five species of rattlesnake, all living in the Americas.
See page 25

## Sailfin Lizards
These lizards live in Indonesia and New Guinea.
See page 31

## Tuatara
There is just one species of tuatara, living only in New Zealand. It is considered an endangered species.
See page 3

Ⓐ
ⒷⒸ

First published in Canada and the United States in 2021

Text and illustration copyright © 2019 Fleurus éditions
This edition copyright © 2021 Pajama Press Inc.
Originally published by Fleurus éditions, Paris, France under the title Quand l'éléphant écoute avec ses pieds...
10 9 8 7 6 5 4 3 2 1

www.pajamapress.ca          info@ pajamapress.ca

 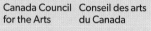  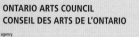

The publisher gratefully acknowledges the support of the Canada Council for the Arts and the Ontario Arts Council for its publishing program. We acknowledge the financial support of the Government of Canada through the Canada Book Fund (CBF) for our publishing activities.

**Library and Archives Canada Cataloguing in Publication**
Title: When elephants listen with their feet : discover extraordinary animal senses / Emmanuelle
   Grundmann; [illustrated by] Clémence Dupont ; translated by Erin Woods.
Other titles: Quand l'éléphant écoute avec ses pieds. English
Names: Grundmann, Emmanuelle, author. | Dupont, Clémence, 1993- illustrator. | Woods, Erin
   (Translator), translator.
Description: Translation of: Quand l'éléphant écoute avec ses pieds.
Identifiers: Canadiana 20200362496 | ISBN 9781772781236 (hardcover)
Subjects: LCSH: Senses and sensation—Juvenile literature. | LCSH: Animals—Juvenile literature.
Classification: LCC QP434 .G7813 2021 | DDC j573.8/7—dc23

**Publisher Cataloging-in-Publication Data (U.S.)**
Names: Grundmann, Emmanuelle, author. | Dupont , Clémence, 1993-, illustrator. | Woods, Erin, translator.
Title: When Elephants Listen With Their Feet / Emmanuelle Grundmann ; Clémence Dupont ; translated by Erin Woods.
Description: Toronto, Ontario Canada : Pajama Press, 2021. | Originally published in French as Quand l'éléphant écoute avec ses
   pieds | Summary: "Chapters focused on the senses of sight, hearing, smell, taste, touch, infrasonic hearing, magnetoception, and
   electroreception detail how a variety of animals experience the world around them, focusing on how their biological adaptations
   to specific ecological niches contribute to senses that often seem extraordinary compared to those of humans. The fully illustrated
   text includes a table of contents, glossary, and index"— Provided by publisher.
Identifiers: ISBN 978-1-77278-123-6 (hardback)

Subjects: LCSH: Senses and sensations -- Juvenile literature. | Animals -- Adaptation -- Juvenile literature. | BISAC: JUVENILE
NONFICTION / Concepts / Senses & Sensation. | JUVENILE NONFICTION / Animals / General. | JUVENILE NONFICTION / Science &
Nature / Zoology.
Classification: LCC QP434.G786 |DDC 612.8 – dc23

Graphics—Bleuenn Auffret
Cover and text—based on original design by Magali Meunier

Printed in China by WKT Company

Pajama Press Inc.
469 Richmond St. E Toronto, ON M5A 1R1

Distributed in Canada by UTP Distribution
5201 Dufferin Street Toronto, Ontario Canada, M3H 5T8

Distributed in the U.S. by Ingram Publisher Services
1 Ingram Blvd. La Vergne, TN 37086, USA